20 FUN FACTS ABOUT FAMOUS TUNNELS

BY KATE LIGHT

 Gareth Stevens
PUBLISHING

Please visit our website, www.garethstevens.com. For a free color catalog of all our high-quality books, call toll free 1-800-542-2595 or fax 1-877-542-2596.

Library of Congress Cataloging-in-Publication Data

Names: Light, Kate, author.
Title: 20 fun facts about famous tunnels / Kate Light.
Other titles: Twenty fun facts about famous tunnels
Description: New York : Gareth Stevens Publishing, [2020] | Series: Fun
  fact file. Engineering marvels | Includes index. | Contents: Dig in! –
  What can tunnels do? – No place like Rome – Creepy catacombs –
  Ancient tunnels – London underground – Into the Holland tunnel –
  Going to great lengths – What's mined is yours – Through the mountains
  – Tunnel visions – Going under.
Identifiers: LCCN 2019030880 | ISBN 9781538246702 (paperback) | ISBN
  9781538246719 (6 Pack)| ISBN 9781538246726 (library binding) | ISBN
  9781538246733 (ebook)
Subjects: LCSH: Tunnels–Miscellanea–Juvenile literature. | CYAC: Tunnels.
  | LCGFT: Instructional and educational works. | Trivia and miscellanea.
Classification: LCC TA807 .L54 2020 | DDC 624.1/93–dc23
LC record available at https://lccn.loc.gov/2019030880

First Edition

Published in 2020 by
Gareth Stevens Publishing
111 East 14th Street, Suite 349
New York, NY 10003

Copyright © 2020 Gareth Stevens Publishing

Designer: Sarah Liddell
Editor: Therese Shea

Photo credits: Cover, p. 1 (main) EQRoy/Shutterstock.com; file folder used throughout David Smart/Shutterstock.com; binder clip used throughout luckyraccoon/Shutterstock.com; wood grain background used throughout ARENA Creative/Shutterstock.com; p. 5 PlusONE/Shutterstock.com; p. 6 Faiz Zaki/Shutterstock.com; p. 7 (natural gas) picture alliance/Contributor/picture alliance/ Getty Images; p. 7 (waste) ALFREDO ESTRELLA/Staff/AFP/Getty Images; p. 7 (water) Peter Gudella/Shutterstock.com; p. 7 (road) asharkyu/Shutterstock.com; p. 7 (railway) TTstudio/Shutterstock.com; p. 7 (canal) iShootEvents/Shutterstock.com; p. 7 (coal mine) Vyacheslav Svetlichnyy/Shutterstock.com; p. 7 (salt mine) Catalin Petolea/Shutterstock.com; p. 7 (diamond mine) Great Siberia Studio/Shutterstock.com; p. 8 kavram/Shutterstock.com; p. 9 Farbregas Hareluya/Shutterstock.com; p. 10 Mikhail Gnatkovskiy/ Shutterstock.com; p. 11 MOHAMED EL-SHAHED/Contributor/AFP/Getty Images; p. 12 Pfeifferfranz/Wikimedia Commons; p. 13 Robert Hoetink/Shutterstock.com; p. 14 UniversalImagesGroup/Contributor/Universal Images Group/Getty Images; p. 15 Science & Society Picture Library/Contributor/SSPL/Getty Images; p. 16 Bettmann/Contributor/Bettmann/Getty Images; p. 17 New York Daily News Archive/Contributor/New York Daily News/Getty Images; p. 18 Matthew Andersen/Shutterstock.com; p. 19 Mortadelo2005/ Wikimedia Commons; pp. 20, 23 Bloomberg/Contributor/Bloomberg/Getty Images; p. 22 CLAUDIO REYES/Contributor/AFP/Getty Images; p. 24 NatalieJean/Shutterstock.com; p. 25 Yuangeng Zhang/Shutterstock.com; p. 26 Karavanov_Lev/Shutterstock.com; p. 27 Yaorusheng/Shutterstock.com; p. 29 Jean-Marc ZAORSKI/Contributor/Gamma-Rapho/Getty Images.

Printed in the United States of America

Some of the images in this book illustrate individuals who are models. The depictions do not imply actual situations or events.

CPSIA compliance information: Batch #CW20GS: For further information contact Gareth Stevens, New York, New York at 1-800-542-2595.

CONTENTS

Words in the glossary appear in **bold** type the first time they are used in the text.

DIG IN!

When you think of the greatest man-made **structures**, you might picture **pyramids** in Egypt or the Eiffel Tower in France. But did you know one of the oldest and most useful forms of building can be found underground?

Tunnels might seem simple, but with them, we've done amazing things. Humans have tunneled deeper into Earth than any other animal, **carved** through mountains, and even traveled underwater! Ready to learn more about the importance of tunnels? Let's dig in!

It's easy to see the usefulness of a tunnel when you walk through an aquarium tunnel. These special structures let you feel like you're walking on the ocean floor.

WHAT CAN TUNNELS DO?

THE SMART TUNNEL IN MALAYSIA IS ENGINEERED FOR *TWO* JOBS.

It's part of a road, and it's a storm **drain** for the rainy season. This tunnel isn't just "smart" because of clever engineering. Its name stands for "Stormwater Management and Road Tunnel."

Malaysia's rainy season, also called monsoon season, leads to flooding. The SMART tunnel of the city of Kuala Lumpur helps move water and control flooding in the streets.

TYPES OF TUNNELS

PUBLIC WORKS

NATURAL GAS

WASTE

WATER

TRANSPORTATION

ROAD

RAILWAY

CANAL

MINING

COAL MINE

SALT MINE

DIAMOND MINE

Mining tunnels reach useful matter deep within the earth. Public works tunnels carry water, waste, and natural gas lines to and from places. Some tunnels are used for transportation, which is the moving of goods and people from place to place.

NO PLACE LIKE ROME

ENGINEERS OF ANCIENT ROME USED GRAVITY TO DRAW WATER INTO THE CITY.

Ancient Romans built **aqueducts** on slopes! Of the 315 miles (507 km) of aqueducts built in Rome, 269 miles (433 km) were underground. The water was for farming, drinking, fountains, and bathing.

Beautiful bridges like this are famous parts of Roman aqueducts. However, they make up less than 12 percent of the aqueduct system, which was built from 312 BC to AD 226.

The Colosseum was used as an amphitheater, which is a round, open theater.

UNDERNEATH THE ROMAN COLOSSEUM, THERE'S A SECRET SYSTEM OF TUNNELS.

Called the hypogeum, these tunnels had wooden lifts to carry animals such as bears and elephants up to a stage! Some tunnels connected to schools for fighters called gladiators as well as other nearby places.

9

CREEPY CATACOMBS

TUNNELS CALLED CATACOMBS WERE USED FOR BURYING THE DEAD!

The catacombs under Paris, France, were first **quarries** that supplied the city with rocks for building. When the city ran out of room to bury people, they moved 6 to 7 million dead bodies into them!

You can visit the catacombs—if you dare—to see bones shaped like hearts, circles, and other shapes!

The catacombs of Kom el Shoqafa are special because they contain carvings and art from the ancient Roman, Greek, and Egyptian **cultures.**

FUN FACT: 5

THE CATACOMBS OF KOM EL SHOQAFA WERE SAID TO HAVE BEEN DISCOVERED BY A DONKEY IN 1900!

A tale says a donkey fell through a hole that leads to these Egyptian tunnels. The catacombs contain a hall called the triclinium where families had feasts to remember their dead.

11

ANCIENT TUNNELS

FUN FACT: 6

THERE ARE MORE THAN 1,000 SIMILAR ANCIENT TUNNELS THROUGHOUT EUROPE — AND NO ONE KNOWS WHAT THEY WERE FOR!

Often called Erdstall tunnels, these mysterious underground tunnels are mostly in Germany and Austria. They're just wide and tall enough for people to move through.

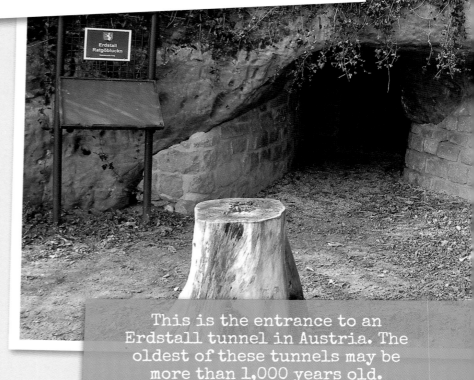

This is the entrance to an Erdstall tunnel in Austria. The oldest of these tunnels may be more than 1,000 years old.

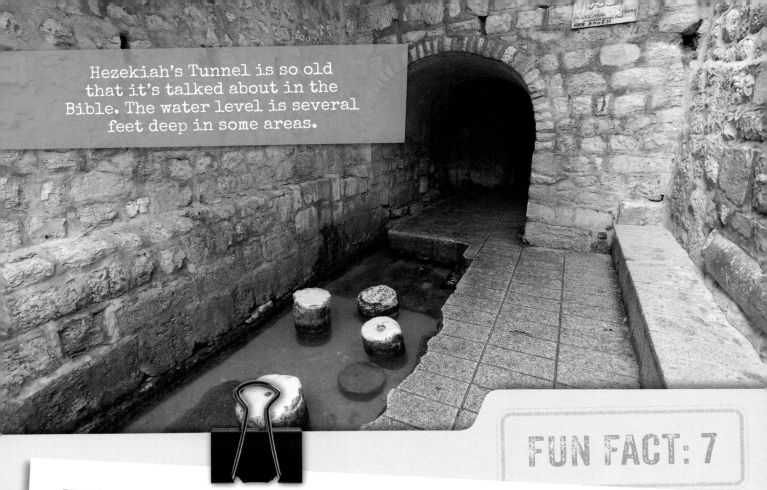

Hezekiah's Tunnel is so old that it's talked about in the Bible. The water level is several feet deep in some areas.

YOU CAN WALK THROUGH A TUNNEL FROM THE 8TH CENTURY BC IN THE MIDDLE EAST — IF YOU DON'T MIND GETTING WET!

Hezekiah's Tunnel was dug to divert, or redirect, water flowing from the Gihon Spring. The tunnel made the spring's water travel into the city of Jerusalem.

LONDON UNDERGROUND

THE FIRST TUNNEL EVER BUILT UNDERWATER WAS THE THAMES TUNNEL IN LONDON, ENGLAND.

People needed to move cargo, or goods, across the Thames River. A bridge would have stopped ships with tall **masts** on the river, so people built a tunnel under the water instead!

Engineer Marc Brunel invented a tunneling shield, or cover, that allowed miners to dig without the tunnel falling down on them.

The Thames Tunnel was called the "Eighth Wonder of the World."

ON THE DAY THE THAMES TUNNEL OPENED, ABOUT 50,000 PEOPLE WALKED THROUGH IT!

Opened in 1843, the tunnel was never successful for cargo transportation. However, people paid to see it—and even sleep in it. It's still part of the London Underground **subway**.

15

INTO THE HOLLAND TUNNEL

ONE OF THE FIRST ROAD TUNNELS EVER BUILT, THE HOLLAND TUNNEL, CARRIES ABOUT 100,000 DRIVERS A DAY!

The tunnel connects New Jersey and New York City. It has one tube for drivers heading east and one for those heading west.

The tunnel opened on November 13, 1927. Cars were backed up for 2 miles (3 km) at first! In just the first hour, 4,047 cars passed through it.

The Holland Tunnel fan system proved itself in 1949 when a truck carrying dangerous matter exploded in the tunnel. No one died because the fans pulled out the poisonous air.

THE HOLLAND TUNNEL IS FAMOUS FOR SOLVING AN IMPORTANT ENGINEERING PROBLEM!

That problem was how to ventilate, or bring fresh air into, a long tunnel. The Holland Tunnel has 84 fans that blow fresh air into the tunnel and take out the polluted air.

THE LONGEST ROAD TUNNEL IN THE WORLD IS 15.2 MILES (24.5 KM) LONG!

The Lærdal Tunnel in Norway takes 20 minutes to drive through. It's filled with special lights that look like daylight so drivers don't fall asleep!

This beautiful tunnel is broken into four parts, each 3.7 miles (6 km) long. Drivers can rest in mountain caves between parts.

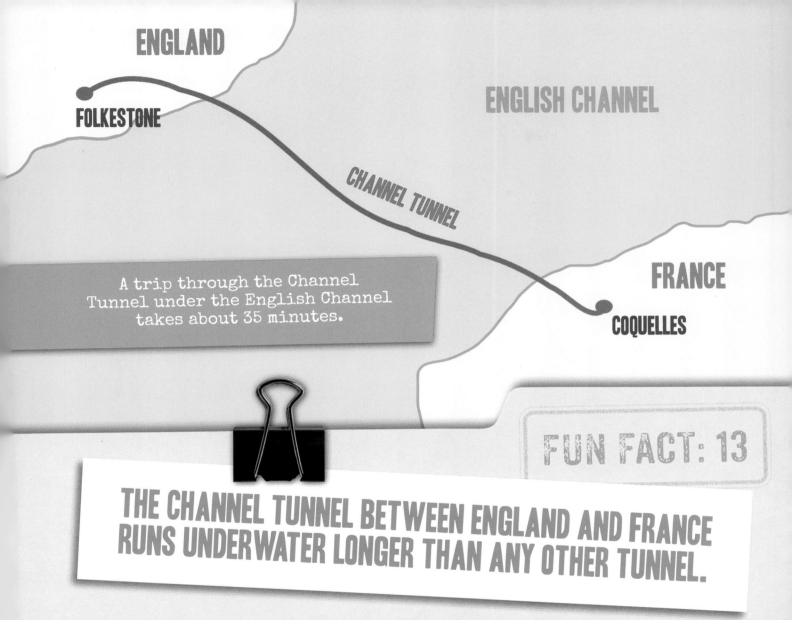

ENGLAND

ENGLISH CHANNEL

FOLKESTONE

CHANNEL TUNNEL

A trip through the Channel Tunnel under the English Channel takes about 35 minutes.

FRANCE

COQUELLES

FUN FACT: 13

THE CHANNEL TUNNEL BETWEEN ENGLAND AND FRANCE RUNS UNDERWATER LONGER THAN ANY OTHER TUNNEL.

Actually three tunnels, the "Chunnel"—as it's often called—is

31 miles (50 km) long. People can either ride a train through it or

ride in their cars, which are placed on trains!

19

It took 17 years to finish the Gotthard Base Tunnel.

THE GOTTHARD BASE TUNNEL IN SWITZERLAND IS THE DEEPEST AND LONGEST RAILWAY TUNNEL.

This tunnel goes as deep as 1.4 miles (2.3 km) below the Swiss Alps and is 35.4 miles (57 km) long. That's longer than 600 football fields!

RECORD-BREAKING TUNNELS

KIND OF TUNNEL	NAME	LOCATION	LENGTH
LONGEST ROAD TUNNEL	LÆRDAL TUNNEL	NORWAY	15.2 MILES (24.5 KM)
LONGEST UNDERSEA TUNNEL SEGMENT	CHANNEL TUNNEL	ENGLISH CHANNEL	31 MILES (50 KM)
LONGEST RAILWAY TUNNEL	GOTTHARD BASE TUNNEL	SWITZERLAND	35.4 MILES (57 KM)
LONGEST SUBWAY TUNNEL	GUANGZHOU METRO LINE 3	CHINA	41 MILES (67 KM)
LONGEST WASTEWATER TUNNEL	EMISOR ORIENTE TUNNEL	MEXICO	38.5 MILES (62 KM)
LONGEST WATER SUPPLY TUNNEL	DELAWARE AQUEDUCT	UNITED STATES	85 MILES (137 KM)

WHAT'S MINED IS YOURS

FUN FACT: 15

THE EL TENIENTE MINE IN CHILE HAS TUNNELS THAT ARE ABOUT THE SAME LENGTH AS THE DISTANCE FROM NEW YORK CITY TO BOULDER, COLORADO!

The El Teniente mine is the largest underground copper mine in the world. It has nearly 932 miles (1,500 km) of underground roads—and a railroad!

El Teniente is located in the Andes Mountains of South America.

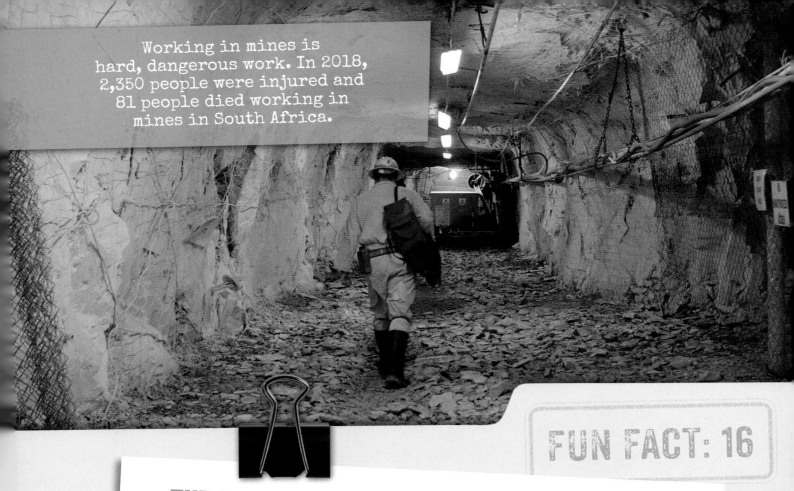

Working in mines is hard, dangerous work. In 2018, 2,350 people were injured and 81 people died working in mines in South Africa.

THE DEEPEST GOLD MINE IN THE WORLD IS OVER 2 MILES (3.2 KM) DEEP!

AngloGold Ashanti's Mponeng gold mine in South Africa gets so close to Earth's core, or center, that it gets as hot as 140°F (60°C). Ice is used to cool off the tunnels!

FUN FACT: 17

THE ZION-MOUNT CARMEL TUNNEL IN UTAH TELLS WORKERS IF A PART IS ABOUT TO FALL IN!

The tunnel goes through a soft kind of rock called sandstone. Although it's made stronger by **concrete**, it has an electric warning system to notify people of weaknesses in the tunnel.

The tunnel gives drivers beautiful views through "windows" in the rock.

The villagers carved the Guoliang Tunnel after the government refused to build a road.

IN CHINA, 13 PEOPLE CARVED A MOUNTAIN TUNNEL *BY HAND!*

Before building this tunnel, the only way the people in Guoliang could get down from their mountain village was a stone staircase with 720 steps called the "Sky Ladder." Tunnel construction took 5 years.

TUNNEL VISIONS

STOCKHOLM'S SUBWAY TUNNELS ARE HOME TO THE LONGEST ART SHOW IN THE WORLD.

More than 90 Stockholm, Sweden, subway stations have been decorated by over 150 artists. There are tours for people interested in learning more about the beautiful art.

The T-Centralen station was the first to be decorated. Artist Per Olof Ultvedt created the blue, flowery paintings in 1975.

This strange journey takes people under the Huangpu River.

THE BUND SIGHTSEEING TUNNEL IN CHINA MAKES PEOPLE FEEL LIKE THEY'RE RIDING FROM SPACE TO THE CENTER OF EARTH!

The tunnel in the city of Shanghai is full of bright, colorful lights and sound effects. People ride through it in a train car with huge windows.

LIFE UNDERGROUND

We can build just about anything underground with the help of tunnels—even a city! The RÉSO is an amazing network of tunnels that make up an "underground city" beneath Montreal, Canada. People can take tunnels to shops, movie theaters, hotels, subway stations, places to eat, and more without ever stepping outside!

What will be the next use for tunnels? Could humans ever live fully underground? Maybe you'll be the next engineer to dig deeper!

This mall and hotel is one of the many buildings connected to Montreal's underground tunnels.

GLOSSARY

aqueduct: a structure that carries water and looks like a bridge

carve: to form by cutting and shaping a material such as stone

concrete: a hard, strong material used for building and made by mixing cement, sand, and broken rocks with water

culture: the beliefs and ways of life of a group of people

distance: the length between two places

drain: a pipe that carries water away from a place

engineer: to use science and math to build better objects. Also, someone who plans and builds machines and other structures.

gravity: the force that pulls objects toward Earth's center

mast: a tall pole that supports a ship's sails

pyramid: a 3-D shape that has a rectangular base and triangular sides

quarry: a place where large amounts of rock or stone are taken out of the ground

structure: something built

subway: a system of underground trains and their tracks

FOR MORE INFORMATION

BOOKS

Graham, Ian. *The Science of Bridges and Tunnels: The Art of Engineering*. New York, NY: Franklin Watts, 2019.

Loh-Hagan, Virginia. *Tunnels*. Ann Arbor, MI: Cherry Lake Publishing, 2017.

Spray, Sally. *Tunnels*. North Mankato, MN: Capstone Press, 2018.

WEBSITES

How Do You Build a Tunnel Underwater?
www.wonderopolis.org/wonder/how-do-you-build-a-tunnel-underwater/
Discover how to build an underwater tunnel!

Transportation
www.brainpop.com/technology/transportation/
Find out about different types of transportation on this fun site.

Tunnels Facts
www.sciencekids.co.nz/sciencefacts/engineering/tunnels.html
Learn more about tunnels on this site which is full of cool facts.

Publisher's note to educators and parents: Our editors have carefully reviewed these websites to ensure that they are suitable for students. Many websites change frequently, however, and we cannot guarantee that a site's future contents will continue to meet our high standards of quality and educational value. Be advised that students should be closely supervised whenever they access the internet.

INDEX